Harry S. Truman
AR RL: 6.9
AR PTS: 1.0
Quiz #: 63031

Harry S. Truman

Childhoods
of the
Presidents

John Adams

George W. Bush

Bill Clinton

Ulysses S. Grant

Andrew Jackson

Thomas Jefferson

John F. Kennedy

Abraham Lincoln

James Madison

James Monroe

Ronald Reagan

Franklin D. Roosevelt

Theodore Roosevelt

Harry S. Truman

George Washington

Woodrow Wilson

Harry S. Truman

Barbara Saffer

Mason Crest Publishers
Philadelphia

Produced by OTTN Publishing, Stockton, New Jersey

Mason Crest Publishers
370 Reed Road
Broomall, PA 19008
www.masoncrest.com

3 5 7 9 8 6 4 2

Library of Congress Cataloging-in-Publication Data

Saffer, Barbara.
    Harry S. Truman / Barbara Saffer.
        p.   cm.   (Childhood of the presidents)
    Summary: A biography of the thirty-third president of the United
    States, focusing on his childhood and young adulthood.
    Includes bibliographical references (p.) and index.
        ISBN 1-59084-282-0
    1. Truman, Harry S., 1884-1972—Childhood and youth—Juvenile
    literature. 2. Truman, Harry S., 1884-1972—Juvenile literature.
    3. Presidents—United States—Biography—Juvenile literature.
    [1. Truman, Harry S., 1884-1972—Childhood and youth. 2.
    Presidents.] I. Title. II. Series.
    E814.S23 2003
    973.918'092—dc21
    [B]   2002069231

Publisher's note: All quotations in this book come from
original sources, and contain the spelling and grammatical
inconsistencies of the original text.

Childhoods
of the
Presidents

Table of Contents

★★★★★★★★★★★★★★★★★

★ *Introduction* ★

Alexis de Tocqueville began his great work *Democracy in America* with a discourse on childhood. If we are to understand the prejudices, the habits and the passions that will rule a man's life, Tocqueville said, we must watch the baby in his mother's arms; we must see the first images that the world casts upon the mirror of his mind; we must hear the first words that awaken his sleeping powers of thought. "The entire man," he wrote, "is, so to speak, to be seen in the cradle of the child."

That is why these books on the childhoods of the American presidents are so much to the point. And, as our history shows, a great variety of childhoods can lead to the White House. The record confirms the ancient adage that every American boy, no matter how unpromising his beginnings, can aspire to the presidency. Soon, one hopes, the adage will be extended to include every American girl.

All our presidents thus far have been white males who, within the limits of their gender, reflect the diversity of American life. They were born in nineteen of our states; eight of the last thirteen presidents were born west of the Mississippi. Of all our presidents, Abraham Lincoln had the least promising childhood, yet he became our greatest president. Oddly enough, presidents who are children of privilege sometimes feel an obligation to reform society in order to give children of poverty a better break. And, with Lincoln the great exception, presidents who are children of poverty sometimes feel that there is no need to reform a society that has enabled them to rise from privation to the summit.

Does schooling make a difference? Harry S. Truman, the only twentieth-century president never to attend college, is generally accounted a near-great president. Actually nine—more than one fifth—of our presidents never went to college at all, including such luminaries as George Washington, Andrew Jackson and Grover Cleveland. But, Truman aside, all the non-college men held the highest office before the twentieth century, and, given the increasing complexity of life, a college education will unquestionably be a necessity in the twenty-first century.

Every reader of this book, girls included, has a right to aspire to the presidency. As you survey the childhoods of those who made it, try to figure out the qualities that brought them to the White House. I would suggest that among those qualities are ambition, determination, discipline, education—and luck.

—ARTHUR M. SCHLESINGER, JR.

Bespectacled, bookish, and polite, the young Harry S. Truman was sometimes a target for teasing. But, a childhood friend recalled, even the tough boys "had a lot of respect for him."

The Buck Stops Here

"We'd be playing cowboy or *shinny*," a childhood friend of the most famous citizen of Independence, Missouri, recalled, ". . . and Harry would come . . . but he did not play much in those rough games because he wore double-strength glasses. He just couldn't get in that kind of a game. But he came by and talked to us."

In a time when it was uncommon for children to wear them, Harry Truman's eyeglasses marked him as a target for other boys' teasing. "Of course, they called me *four-eyes* and a lot of other things, too. That's hard on a boy. It makes him lonely," Harry remembered years later.

The young Harry Truman also exposed himself to teasing by taking piano lessons, considered a "girl's activity" among the boys of Independence. But Harry loved music, and he wasn't about to let *peer pressure* get in the way of doing something he enjoyed. As his close friend Charlie Ross explained, "It required a lot of courage for a kid to take music lessons in a town like Independence."

Perhaps it was because they could sense this courage that the rowdy boys accepted the polite and bookish kid who never joined their rough sports and games. Perhaps they admired the inner strength that allowed Harry Truman to stay true to himself. "They wanted to call him a sissy," childhood friend Henry P. Chiles remembered, "but they just didn't do it because they had a lot of respect for him."

As an adult, Harry Truman would win the respect of millions of Americans—including many of his opponents—by having the courage to do what he thought was right, regardless of how a decision might affect him personally or whether it was politically popular. The boy whose glasses had prevented him from joining in the rough games of his peers put himself in harm's way as a man by joining the army during World War I—even though his poor eyesight could have excused him from having to fight in that deadly conflict.

Truman grew up in a region of Missouri that had supported slavery during the *Civil War* and that continued to treat African Americans as second-class citizens. Yet when he became president, he *integrated* the U.S. armed forces and urged Congress to pass civil rights legislation for blacks, saying, "We shall not . . . achieve the ideals for which this nation was founded so long as any American suffers *discrimination*." This so angered Truman's fellow Democrats from the South that many left the Democratic Party, organized the States' Rights Party (also known as the "Dixiecrats"), and fielded a candidate to run against Truman in the 1948 presidential election. Surprising almost everyone, Truman beat both the Dixiecrat nominee and the heavily favored Republican candidate, Thomas Dewey, to win another term.

Another courageous decision that Truman made was to

Nearly everyone had counted Harry Truman out during the 1948 presidential campaign. The *Chicago Daily Tribune* even declared Thomas Dewey the winner before the election results were in—but Truman got the last laugh.

fire General Douglas MacArthur during the Korean War. MacArthur, the supreme commander of the U.S.-led forces fighting the **Communists** in Korea, was an extremely popular figure with the American people and had many supporters in Congress. He'd been a hero of World War II and had planned the daring—and successful—Inchon invasion during the early months of the fighting in Korea. But Truman felt that MacArthur had been ignoring his instructions, and in the United States the president is commander in chief of all the armed forces. To protect this important idea, the president dismissed MacArthur. The outcry was enormous.

But Harry Truman never made excuses or apologized for doing what he thought needed to be done. On his desk in the Oval Office in the White House was a sign that summed up his attitude. It read, The Buck Stops Here—meaning Truman himself took responsibility for the actions of his administration, and if anyone wanted to blame someone for a particular decision, they could blame him.

Harry Truman, age four, with his brother Vivian, age two, 1888. Harry would later say, "I had just the happiest childhood that could ever be imagined."

"The Happiest Childhood"

On May 8, 1884, Martha Ellen Young Truman gave birth to her first child, a baby boy. As was customary in those days, the birth occurred not in a hospital, but in the home Martha shared with her husband, John Anderson Truman. The couple named their son Harry S. Truman (the middle initial stood for no actual name).

To celebrate Harry's arrival, John Truman planted a pine tree in the front yard of his homestead, which was located in the small Missouri village of Lamar, population about 700. The tree still grows there. Legend says that, for good luck, John also nailed a horseshoe over the front door. The house, now a state historic site, displays such a horseshoe today. When the Trumans lived in it the small, white structure had no electricity, running water, or indoor plumbing.

In many respects Harry Truman's parents were quite different. John Truman, who had been educated in a country school, made his living as a farmer and animal trader. Though gentle with his family, he had a bad temper and, as his son later recalled, "fought like a buzz saw" when he felt someone had insulted him.

By contrast, Martha Truman—called Mattie by her family and friends—was refined and well educated. Before her marriage, she had studied art and music at the Baptist Female College in Lexington, Missouri. Despite the fact that she was the daughter of farmers and had married a farmer, Mattie somehow managed to avoid farm work throughout her life. She never learned to milk a cow, saying: "Papa told me that if I never learned, I'd never have to do it." Mattie rarely even cooked, except for her favorite dish: fried chicken. Like her husband, though, she had strong opinions and was accustomed to speaking her mind.

The Truman family moved several times while Harry was a baby. When he was one, the family moved to Harrisonville, Missouri. Harry's oldest recollection was himself as a two-year-old, chasing a frog around the yard of the Harrisonville home. Watching the show, Harry's grandmother was delighted at the way Harry slapped his knees and laughed at the jumping frog.

In 1887, when Harry was three, the Trumans moved in with Mattie's parents, Solomon and Harriet Young. By this time Harry had a baby brother, John Vivian (called Vivian), born in April 1886. Harry's sister, Mary Jane, was born in August 1889.

The Young farm, 17 miles south of Kansas City, was called Grandview. The farmhouse was not large, but Grandview included 600 acres of land. Harry and Vivian had wonderful times there. They ran through the bluegrass of the farmstead's south lawn and raced their red wagon on the house's long north porch. They searched for birds' nests, picked wild straw-

Harry's parents, Martha Ellen "Mattie" Young Truman and John Anderson Truman, sat for this wedding portrait on December 28, 1881. Though quite different in many respects, they shared at least one trait: they both were accustomed to speaking their mind.

berries, and played on swings—one under an old elm tree and another in the front hall, for rainy days.

Harry had a gray cat named Bob and a little black and tan dog named Tandy. He loved to romp through the prairie grass and cornfields with these pets, and later said, "I had just the happiest childhood that could ever be imagined."

Harry especially loved spending time with Grandpa Young, who doted on him. One of Harry's favorite memories was of accompanying Grandpa Young to the Cass County Fair in Belton, Missouri, in 1889. Grandpa Young was a judge for the horse races, and—every day for a week—took Harry to the fair in a horse-drawn cart. Harry and his grandfather sat together in the judges' stand while Harry ate candy and watched the races.

Harry also had wonderful memories of his uncle Harrison Young. Uncle Harrison lived in Kansas City and brought toys and candy whenever he visited. Harrison told funny stories and taught Harry to play checkers, chess, and card games. Later, Harry remembered, "When [Uncle Harrison] came it was just like Christmas."

Harry spent time with other relatives as well. His aunt Mary Martha Truman came for long visits, and another aunt, Ada Young, often played games with him. Harry was part of a large, warm-hearted family in which all kinfolk—no matter how distantly related—were welcome at any time.

At Grandview, John Truman gave Harry a black Shetland pony and a saddle and let his son ride along when he inspected the farm. Father and son surveyed poultry, horses, cattle, crops, and more. Later, Harry wrote: "I became familiar with every sort of animal on the farm, and watched the wheat harvest, the threshing and the corn shucking, mowing and stacking hay, and every evening at suppertime heard my father tell a dozen farmhands what to do."

Harry also remembered the delicious food at Grandview. In autumn, Harry watched Grandmother Young and her helpers prepare dried apples, dried peaches, grape butter, apple butter, peach butter, jellies, and preserves. In late fall, after the pigs were slaughtered, the women extracted fat, or lard, in a huge iron kettle. Sausages and pickled pigs' feet were

Harry Truman's mother once said, "It was on the farm that Harry got his common sense. He didn't get it in town."

Harry Truman was born in this small house in Lamar, Missouri, on May 8, 1884. John Truman planted the pine tree at left to mark the happy occasion.

prepared as well, to go with corn pudding and roast corn. Grandmother Young also made fabulous pies, cookies, and candies.

John and Martha Truman were strict with their children and expected them to behave well. Like all youngsters, though, Harry sometimes got into trouble. One day, Harry, Vivian, and a neighbor boy named John Chancellor were playing near a mud hole in the south pasture. Harry packed Vivian and John into his little red wagon, towed them into the mud hole, and turned the wagon over. Harry's mother was furious, and she punished only him because she believed the mischief had been his idea. "What a spanking I received," Harry remembered. "I can feel it yet! Every stitch of clothes on all three of us had to be changed, scrubbed and dried, and so did we."

Although he never spanked his children, Harry's father was stern, too. One day, Harry fell off his pony while riding behind his father on the farm. John Truman said a boy who could not stay on a pony should walk home. Harry cried as he trudged the half mile back to the house. Martha Truman felt the punishment was too harsh, but Harry thought his father was right. He later wrote, "Mamma thought I was badly mis-

Interior of Harry Truman's birthplace, which had no electricity, running water, or indoor plumbing.

treated but I wasn't, in spite of my crying all the way to the house. I learned a lesson."

Harry had wonderful memories of Grandview, but there were bad times as well. Grandfather Truman, who had sold his farm and gone to

In the 1950s, the United Automobile Workers union bought the house in which Harry Truman was born for $6,000. The home was restored and later donated to the state of Missouri.

live with the family, died shortly after moving to Grandview. Three-year-old Harry pulled the old man's beard, trying to wake him up. Another time, Harry climbed up on a chair to comb his hair in front of a mirror. He lost his balance and tumbled over backward, breaking his collarbone. Even worse, Harry almost choked to death when a peach pit got stuck in his throat. Mattie rushed over and pushed the pit down his throat, saving her son's life.

While the Trumans were living on the Young farm, Harry's mother realized her son had eye trouble. Before Harry was five, Martha Truman had taught him to read using the large print in the family Bible. Martha noticed, though, that Harry couldn't see distant objects, like a buggy bumping down the road or a cow across the pasture.

Martha's concerns reached a high point during a Fourth of July celebration in 1890, when Harry was six. Harry jumped at the sound of the fireworks, but he couldn't see them. Shortly afterward, Harry's mother took her son to Kansas City to see an eye doctor. Revealing that Harry suffered from "flat eyeballs," the doctor prescribed double-strength spectacles.

One of the homes in Independence, Missouri, in which Harry Truman lived. Mattie insisted that the family move to Independence when Harry was six because she wanted her children to attend good schools.

To Independence

*I*n 1890, Martha Truman decided that her family should move to Independence, Missouri. Mattie wanted her children to get a good education, and Independence—10 miles east of Kansas City—had fine public schools. Independence was also an attractive place. The main streets were clean and paved, and people had charming homes and lovely gardens. Independence was also a cultured city, where people read books and newspapers, discussed current events, and enjoyed picnics, hayrides, and parties.

In many ways, though, Independence resembled a city of the old South. Its citizens maintained strong emotional ties to the *Confederacy*. (The Confederacy was the name given to the states that seceded, or withdrew from, the United States over the issue of slavery and fought the Union during the Civil War.) Citizens of Independence visited a local Confederate monument, waved handkerchiefs when a band played "Dixie" (a popular song of the South), and hung portraits of the South's heroes in their parlors. In addition, people in Independence honored the memory of Quantrill's Raiders, a ferocious band of Missouri *bushwhackers* that attacked Union

In 1849, Independence, Missouri, was a jumping-off place for thousands of pioneers traveling west during the California gold rush.

supporters during the Civil War.

Many Independence residents were originally from Virginia and Kentucky, and had been slaveholders before the Civil War. They resented free blacks and barred them from local shops. Black people were forced to live in a separate community—composed of huts in a persimmon grove—and had their own school. Blacks who "forgot their place" risked violent attack.

Though close to Kansas City, Independence remained a country town in some ways. The town square filled up with wagons on Saturday nights, when farmers drove in for supplies; most people ate their main meal at noon; and city residents did "farm tasks" every day. Harry remembered, "[I had to] carry the milk to the house, and put it in a cooler so I could have milk for breakfast. . . . I had to wash the dishes, and wash the lamp chimneys, so that we could have clean dishes for the next meal, and for light. . . . I had to split wood and carry it and put it in the woodbox behind the stove, so I could get up in the morning and start a fire so that we could have breakfast."

In 1890, when they first moved to Independence, the Trumans bought a home on Crysler Avenue. The white clapboard house, topped by a *cupola* with a rooster weathervane, came with several acres of land. John Truman used part of the land to grow strawberries and vegetables, and the rest for his animal business. John bought and sold goats, sheep, cows, and horses. Long afterward, Harry remembered his father using a horse-drawn wagon to take lambs and calves from Independence to the stockyards in Kansas City.

The Truman house was near the Missouri Pacific Railroad Station, and when trains rumbled past, dishes clattered and soot wafted in. Harry loved to watch the trains, though, and often perched on the roof of the coal shed behind the house to count freight cars.

John Truman prospered in Independence. The extra money allowed him to buy a special gift for his children: a miniature farm wagon pulled by a pair of goats. The Truman children had other pets as well, including ponies, dogs, cats, pigeons, and pigs. Neighborhood youngsters often gathered at the Truman house, and Harry always remembered how much fun they had. In later years, he wrote, "With our barns, chicken house, and a grand yard in which to play, all the boys and girls in the neighborhood for blocks around congregated at our house. We always had ponies and horses to ride, goats to hitch to our little wagon. . . . We would harness two red goats to the little wagon and drive it everywhere around the place."

John's success in the animal business also allowed the Trumans to purchase books (which Harry loved), go to a portrait studio for family pictures, and hire domestic help for the housework that Mattie so disliked. To assist with the cooking and washing, Mattie hired a black woman named Caroline Simpson. Caroline, her husband Letch, and their four children lived with the Trumans. Harry liked to linger in the warm, cozy

When Harry Truman was a child, citizens of Independence considered nearby Kansas City a shameless "Yankee town."

kitchen, chatting with Caroline and watching her cook on the big wood stove. Harry also enjoyed taking care of his baby sister, Mary Jane, who was one year old in 1890. He would rock Mary Jane for hours, fix her hair, and sing her to sleep.

Harry recalled one awful experience at the Crysler Avenue house, when the cellar door slammed on his foot and cut off the end of his big toe. Martha Truman dashed over, found the cut section, and held it in place until the doctor arrived. The doctor attached the segment, applied medicine, and bandaged Harry's foot.

As soon as the Trumans moved to Independence, Martha Truman enrolled her eldest child in Sunday school. The Trumans were Baptists, but because Mattie liked the Presbyterian minister, she registered Harry in the Presbyterian church's Sunday school.

In Sunday school Harry met a little girl named Elizabeth Virginia Wallace. A spunky tomboy, Elizabeth was called Bessie by her family and friends. The young Harry immediately liked Bessie, but he was shy around her. Years later, though, she would become Harry's sweetheart and then his wife. Long afterward, Harry wrote, "When my mother started us to Sunday school she gave us a chance to meet the other children in Independence. I met a very beautiful little lady with lovely blue eyes and the prettiest golden curls I've ever seen. We went through Sunday school, grade school, high school and we're still going along hand in hand. She was my sweetheart and ideal when I was a little boy—and she still is."

In the fall of 1892, when Harry Truman was eight, he started elementary school at the Noland School. Harry enjoyed

Harry Truman is in the front row at the far left in this second-grade class picture from the Noland School in Independence.

school and particularly liked his first-grade teacher, Miss Mira Ewing. Later, he recalled, "That first year in school made a profound impression on me. I learned to get along with my classmates and also learned a lot from Appleton's First Reader, learned how to add and subtract, and stood in well with my teacher." Harry often said that the influence of teachers on his life was second only to that of his mother. "I do not remember a bad teacher in all my experience," he claimed. Teachers liked Harry also. He was a good student, had a cheerful personality, and was courteous to everyone he met.

Harry's schooling was stalled in January 1894 when he caught diphtheria, a severe infection with dangerous side

A statue of Independence's favorite son stands before the courthouse.

HARRY S. TRUMAN
1884 – 1972
PRESIDENT
OF THE
UNITED STATES
1945 – 1953

effects. He was doctored with *ipecac* and whiskey, and hated the smell of both for the rest of his life. Despite the treatment, though, his arms, legs, and throat became paralyzed. For months, as Harry recovered, his mother pushed him around in a baby carriage.

When Harry was well enough, he was tutored at home. He not only kept up with his schoolwork, he leaped ahead. When he returned to school in the fall of 1894, he skipped a grade, to fourth grade. From fourth through seventh grade, Harry attended a newly built school, the Columbian School.

Harry got good grades in elementary school, mostly 90s and some 100s. His best subjects were math and English. Throughout his life, Harry loved to read, and by the time he was 12 he'd read the Bible twice. He also spent a great deal of time at the Independence Public Library. He claimed to have read every book in the library, including the encyclopedias. Harry especially enjoyed the works of Shakespeare and Plutarch's *Lives*, biographies of famous Greeks and Romans. In fact, Harry's favorite books were about leading historical figures.

On his 10th birthday, his mother gave him a set of illustrated books titled *Great Men and Famous Women*, by Charles Francis Horne. The four books—*Soldiers and Sailors*; *Statesmen and Sages*; *Workmen and Heroes*; and *Artists and Authors*—sparked Harry's interest in history. Later, Harry said this marked a turning point in his life. He wrote, "Readers of good books, particularly books of biography and history, are preparing themselves for leadership. Not all readers become leaders. But all leaders must be readers."

Harry especially liked *Soldiers and Sailors*. His heroes were the great military leaders of history, including Cincinnatus, Scipio, Hannibal, Cyrus the Great, and Gustavus Adolphus. Harry also admired President Andrew Jackson and General Robert E. Lee.

In 1896, when Harry was almost 12, the Trumans moved to a more fashionable part of Independence. They bought a house on Waldo Avenue, not far from Courthouse Square. The courthouse, an impressive building with a clock tower five stories tall, was in the center of the business district. This contained a hotel, a dancing school, a jewelry store, a

Harry Truman was the last American president who was not a college graduate.

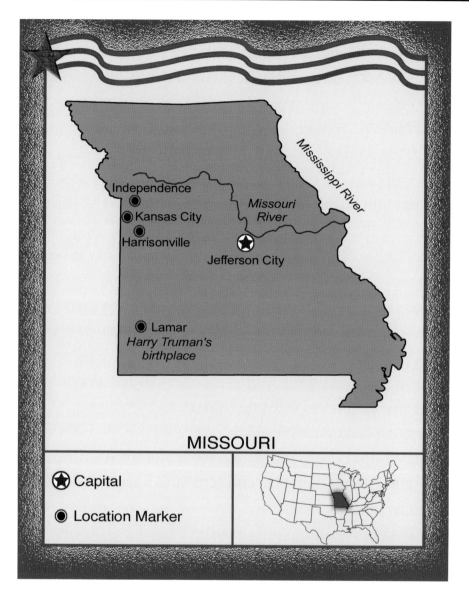

This map of Missouri shows the towns where the Truman family lived during Harry's childhood.

bookshop, a saddle shop, a hardware store, a theater, an opera house, a bakery, a department store, an ice cream parlor, banks, law offices, dental offices, grocery stores, drugstores, barbershops, *saloons*, and other businesses.

In addition to being near all these attractions, the Waldo Avenue home had another advantage in Harry's view: it was close to North Delaware Street, where Bessie Wallace's family lived. Harry had admired Bessie since the age of six, when he first met her in Sunday school. But he was shy with girls and didn't talk to Bessie until five years later, when they were in elementary school. Harry and Bessie were classmates, and sometimes walked to school together. Later, Harry wrote, "If I succeeded in carrying her books to school and back home for her I had a big day." Harry and Bessie didn't often meet outside school, though, because their families belonged to different social circles. The Wallaces were wealthy, and their street was among the most elegant in town. The Trumans were of much more modest means.

Still, there were lots of youngsters in the neighborhood, and the Truman house often served as their gathering place. Harry recalled, "Our house became headquarters for all the boys and girls around. . . . There was a wonderful barn with stalls for horses and cows, a corn crib and a hayloft in which all kids met and cooked up plans for all sorts of adventures."

Harry and his friends also liked to play "army." When the Spanish-American War broke out in 1898, Harry and a group of teenage boys formed a .22-caliber rifle company called the Independence Junior *Militia*. Later, Harry wrote, "In the Spanish-American War we organized a .22 rifle company, elected a captain and marched and countermarched, camped out in the woods just a block or two north of our house, and had a grand time. Not one of the boys was over fourteen."

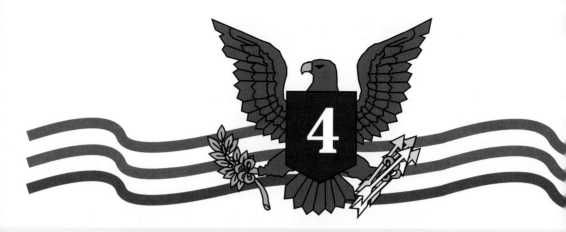

Independence High School's class of 1901. Harry Truman is in the back row, fourth from left. His future wife, Bess Wallace, sits in the second row at right, and Charlie Ross, his best friend and future press secretary, is in the front row at left.

Dreams and Setbacks

When the Trumans moved to their home on Waldo Avenue, they bought a piano for the parlor. Harry began taking lessons, first from his mother, then from a local piano teacher. He displayed great talent for the instrument and eventually mastered everything the local instructor could teach him. So, Harry began traveling to Kansas City to take lessons once or twice a week with a talented pianist named Grace White.

Harry practiced two hours every day without fail. He loved classical music and enjoyed playing works by Bach, Beethoven, Chopin, Mozart, and others. Harry also attended concerts at every opportunity. Once, Grace White took him backstage after a concert to meet the famous Polish musician Ignace Paderewski. Harry had been having trouble learning to play a section of Paderewski's Minuet in G, and the *renowned* pianist took several minutes to show the eager boy. It was an experience Harry never forgot.

Harry Truman became a fine musician. He may even have fulfilled his dream to become a concert pianist had his father not suffered a large financial setback after Harry had graduated from high school. This forced him to give up studying the instrument in favor of finding a steady job.

Harry got his first job in 1898, when he was 14. He worked at J. H. Clinton's Drugstore, which sold toiletries, ice cream, soda, candy, medicine, and other supplies. Harry opened the store at 6:30 A.M., before going to school. He also worked afternoons and weekends, making ice cream, helping out behind the soda fountain, emptying trash, sweeping the floor, washing windows, dusting bottles, and doing other small tasks. Harry earned three silver dollars for his first week of work. He bought a gift for his mother and tried to give the rest to his father, who told Harry to keep the money for himself. Harry left the job after three months, though, because his parents wanted him to concentrate on his schoolwork.

Harry graduated from the Columbian School in 1898, after the seventh grade. He went on to Independence High School along with Bessie Wallace and his old friend Charlie Ross. Few boys in Independence attended high school in the 1890s. Harry's class had 30 girls and just 11 boys. Their high school courses included history, math, English, Latin, and science.

Harry was smart, but he was not the brightest student in the class. That honor went to Charlie Ross, who later became Harry's presidential press secretary. During their senior year in high school, Harry and Charlie published a school magazine, *The Gleam*. Both boys liked Latin, and they translated works by

In a high school composition, Harry Truman once wrote, "A true heart, a strong mind, and a great deal of courage, and I think a man will get through the world."

"His appearance is good and his habits and character are of the best," a supervisor wrote in a job evaluation of bank clerk Harry Truman, whom he also called "an exceptionally bright young man" and "a willing worker" who "tries hard to please everybody."

Cicero—a statesman in ancient Rome—for the magazine.

Harry graduated from high school in 1901, when he was 17. As a graduation gift, his parents sent him to visit relatives in St. Louis, Missouri, and Murphysboro, Illinois. Harry had a marvelous time, but bad news greeted him when he returned home. Because of unwise investments, John Truman had lost all of the family's money and land. Later, Harry recalled, "He got the notion he could get rich. Instead he lost everything at one fell swoop and went completely broke."

There was no way Harry's parents could afford to send him to college now. And his applications to the United States Military Academy at West Point and the United States Naval Academy at Annapolis—where he could get a free educa-tion—had already been rejected because of his poor eyesight.

Harry Truman shares a rowboat with Bess Wallace (holding fishing pole), two female relatives of hers, and an unidentified man, August 1913. Harry had first proposed marriage to Bess two years earlier, but it would be 1917 before she finally agreed to be his wife.

Still, Harry's parents wanted him to get some job skills. So, in the fall of 1901, Harry enrolled in a business school called Spaulding's Commercial College. Every day, Harry took a streetcar from Independence to Kansas City to attend classes.

Unfortunately, the Trumans' financial problems worsened. They were forced to sell their home and move to Kansas City in 1902. There, John Truman got work as a night watchman at a *grain elevator*. Harry quit school and gave up his piano lessons so he could work and help the family.

For a short time, Harry worked in the mailroom of the

Kansas City Star newspaper. Then, in the summer of 1902, he got a job as timekeeper for the Santa Fe Railroad. Harry's job was to keep a record of the hours worked by the men, mostly hobos, who were laying down new tracks. Every morning, Harry pumped a handcart down 10 miles of rail to make lists of the men working at different construction sites. In the afternoon, he did the same thing, to make sure the men were still working. Every two weeks, Harry gave out paychecks.

Harry worked 10 hours a day, six days a week, for $30 a month plus board. He ate and slept in tent camps with the railroad crews. There, he learned about the problems of poor people. Later, Harry said that the men "taught me many, many things that had been a closed book to me up to this time," and that he "received a very down-to-earth education in the handling of men." Harry worked for the railroad for six months, until the new tracks were completed.

In 1903, when Harry was almost 19, he got a job as a clerk in the National Bank of Commerce in Kansas City. There, he cleared checks drawn on numerous country banks, and handled up to a million dollars a day. On Harry's job evaluation, the chief clerk, A. D. Flinton, wrote, "an exceptionally bright young man . . . He is a willing worker, almost always here and tries hard to please everybody. . . . He watches everything very closely and by his watchfulness, detects many errors which a careless boy would let slip through. His appearance is good and his habits and character are of the best." Harry earned 20 dollars a month when he began at the National Bank of Commerce, and 40 dollars a month after two years. Harry then took a higher-paying job with another bank.

Road to the White House

H arry Truman was 22 when his father took over management of the Young farm in 1906. To help his father, Harry quit his bank job and joined the family at Grandview. When John Truman died in 1914, Harry took over as farm manager. Afterward, Harry tried other jobs. He invested in a zinc mine and an oil company, and was part owner of a men's clothing store. These ventures were not successful, however.

Harry also joined the Missouri National Guard. He enlisted in 1905, served for six years, and left as a corporal.

During this time, Harry stayed in touch with Bessie Wallace, who was now called Bess. One day in 1910, while visiting relatives in Independence, he stopped by her house. From then on, Harry was Bess's *beau*. He wrote her often and visited when he could. Harry first proposed marriage to Bess in a letter in 1911. Bess refused, but Harry persisted. Finally, in

Grim expressions abound as Harry Truman takes the presidential oath of office, April 12, 1945. Earlier in the day, Franklin D. Roosevelt had died suddenly. Many people, including some of Roosevelt's aides, believed Truman unprepared to assume the presidency, but historians generally agree that he acquitted himself quite well.

Harry Truman was 22 when he sat for this photo in his National Guard uniform. Truman believed someone going into politics needed experience in three fields: finance, farming, and the military.

1917, Bess agreed to become Harry's wife.

America's entry into World War I put the couple's wedding plans on hold. Harry enlisted in the army and was sent to France, where he became captain of an *artillery unit*. Harry won the respect of his men because he genuinely seemed to care about them and was very careful with their lives. In fact, not a single member of the unit Harry commanded was killed in battle. In May 1919, Harry was discharged from the army. He married Bess the following month. Their only child, a daughter named Mary Margaret, was born in 1924.

By that time, Harry had been active in the Democratic Party for some time. In 1922, with the help of powerful Democrats in Kansas City, he'd won election to the position of judge of Jackson County. This was not a court post, but involved overseeing public-works projects, such as roads, that could involve millions of dollars. Corruption had long been a hallmark of the position: judges in Jackson County and elsewhere in Missouri often skimmed some of the public funds for themselves or their families and friends. Harry, by contrast, won a reputation for honesty and efficiency as a judge.

In 1935, Harry was elected to the U.S. Senate. In 1941, he gained national recognition for heading a Senate committee that investigated defense spending. (World War II had been raging in Europe for two years, and the United States would be drawn into the conflict by the end of the year, after Japan attacked the U.S. naval base at Pearl Harbor.) The panel, called the Truman Committee, uncovered massive waste and fraud, saving the government $15 billion. Harry won the respect of many Americans, and in 1944 President Franklin D. Roosevelt selected him as his vice presidential running mate. Roosevelt was seeking his fourth term as president.

Roosevelt won the election, and Harry became vice president. But just 83 days after assuming that position, he was thrust into a much more important role. On April 12, 1945, Roosevelt died. That evening, Harry took the oath of office and became president. The next day, he told reporters, "Boys, if you ever pray, pray for me now. I don't know whether you fellows ever had a load of hay fall on you, but when they told me yesterday what had happened, I felt like the moon, the stars, and all the planets had fallen on me."

As president, Harry Truman made some of the most important decisions in history. In the summer of 1945, he ordered the dropping of atomic bombs on Japan to end World War II. The bombs destroyed the cities of Hiroshima and Nagasaki, killing at least 200,000 Japanese. Though he was often criticized for unleashing the atomic bombs, Truman always insisted that it had been the right decision because it had saved the lives of tens of thousands of American soldiers.

America's 33rd president with the Soviet Union's premier, Joseph Stalin (front, left), at the Potsdam Conference, July 18, 1945. Wartime allies, the United States and the Soviet Union soon became bitter adversaries, and Truman crafted a foreign policy designed to contain the spread of Soviet-sponsored communism.

Shortly after World War II ended, the United States and its wartime ally the Soviet Union had a falling-out. The Soviets, it seemed, were determined to spread *communism* around the world. Within a few years all of Eastern Europe was firmly in their grasp. To prevent the rest of Europe—and other areas of the world—from becoming Communist, President Truman announced the Truman Doctrine, which promised that America would help nations resist communism; set up the Marshall Plan to rebuild war-torn Europe; and helped establish the North Atlantic Treaty Organization (NATO), a military pact among Western European nations and the United States. He also sent American troops to South Korea in 1950, to repel an attack by Communist North Korea.

In 1948, President Truman boldly recognized the new state of Israel, which has since then been America's strongest ally in the Middle East. That same year, he became the first president to ask Congress to pass civil rights legislation for African Americans.

In November 1948, Truman was elected to another term in office. During his second term, he introduced a program called the Fair Deal, to help "average" American citizens. Among other things, the program called for national health insurance, federal aid for education, more public housing, higher wages, conservation measures, broader social security, and more support for farmers.

President Truman left office in 1953 and returned to his home in Independence, Missouri. He died on December 26, 1972, and was buried in the Truman Library courtyard in Independence. Many historians rank Harry Truman as one of the 10 best American presidents.

Harry Truman in retirement at his home in Independence. The former president never forgot his roots and remained a plain-speaking, unassuming man until the end of his days.

CHRONOLOGY

1884 Harry S. Truman is born in Lamar, Missouri.

1887 Moves to Grandview, the farm owned by mother's parents.

1890 Gets eyeglasses; moves to Independence, Missouri.

1892 Enters elementary school.

1894 Contracts diphtheria and is partially paralyzed for a while.

1896 Begins piano lessons.

1898 Gets a job at J. H. Clinton's Drugstore; begins high school.

1901 Graduates from high school; enrolls in Spaulding's Commercial College after family goes bankrupt.

1902 Quits school, gives up piano lessons, and goes to work for the Santa Fe Railroad.

1903 Gets a job with the National Bank of Commerce in Kansas City.

1905 Joins the Missouri National Guard.

1906 Moves back to Grandview and becomes a farmer.

1917–1919 Serves in the army as an artillery captain.

1919 Marries Bess Wallace.

1922 Becomes judge (an administrative, not a legal, position) in Jackson County, Missouri.

1924 Daughter, Mary Margaret, is born.

1935 Becomes a United States senator.

1944 Becomes vice president.

1945 Becomes president when Franklin Delano Roosevelt dies; orders that atomic bombs be dropped on Japan.

1947–1949 Announces the Truman Doctrine and the Marshall Plan, and helps set up NATO.

1948 Is elected to another term as president; recognizes Israel; asks Congress to pass civil rights legislation; introduces the Fair Deal.

1950 Sends American soldiers to fight Communists in Korea.

1953 Leaves office.

1972 Dies and is buried in Independence, Missouri.

artillery unit—a military group that uses large-caliber weapons and rocket launchers in support of infantry, or foot soldiers.

beau—a boyfriend.

bushwhacker—a fighter (especially a supporter of the Confederacy during the Civil War) who is not part of a regular army and who uses guerrilla tactics such as ambushes in attacking the enemy.

Civil War—the war in the United States between the North, or Union, and the South, or Confederacy, fought between 1861 and 1865 over the issues of slavery and states' rights.

communism—a political system in which the government controls the production and distribution of goods.

Communist—a person or country that believes in and promotes communism.

Confederacy—a group of 11 southern states that seceded, or withdrew, from the United States in 1860 and 1861, leading to the Civil War.

cupola—a small dome on a roof.

discrimination—unfair treatment of people based only on a characteristic such as race.

grain elevator—a storehouse for grain.

integrate—to bring members of all races into a group or organization.

ipecac—a medicine that induces vomiting.

militia—a nonprofessional, volunteer group of soldiers, usually drawn from the same geographical area.

peer pressure—pressure from one's age group or circle of friends to do something one doesn't really want to do.

renowned—famous or celebrated.

saloon—a place where liquor and beer are served; a bar.

shinny—a game that resembles hockey and is played with a curved stick and a ball or block of wood.

FURTHER READING

Collins, David R. *Harry S. Truman, People's President*. New York: Chelsea House Publishers, 1991.

Farley, Karin C. *Harry Truman: The Man from Independence*. New York: Simon & Schuster, 1989.

Ferrell, Robert H. *Harry S. Truman: A Life*. Columbia: University of Missouri Press, 1994.

Hargrove, Jim. *Encyclopedia of Presidents: Harry S. Truman*. Chicago: Children's Press, 1987.

McCullough, David. *Truman*. New York: Simon & Schuster, 1992.

Poen, Monte M., ed. *Letters Home by Harry Truman*. Boston: G. K. Hall & Co., 1984.

Schuman, Michael A. *United States Presidents: Harry S. Truman*. Springfield, N.J.: Enslow Publishers, 1997.

Truman, Harry S. *The Autobiography of Harry S. Truman*. Ed. by Robert H. Ferrell. Boulder: Colorado Associated University Press, 1980.

Truman, Margaret. *Harry S. Truman*. New York: William Morrow & Company, 1972.

- http://www.americanpresident.org/history/harrytruman
  The American President website for Harry Truman

- http://www.trumanlibrary.org/
  The Truman Presidential Museum and Library

- http://www.pbs.org/wgbh/amex/president/33_truman/
  The PBS series *American Experience* program on Harry Truman, including special features

- http://www.mostateparks.com/trumansite.htm
  Harry S. Truman Birthplace State Historic Site

- http://www.americanpresidents.org/presidents/president.asp?president-number=32
  C-SPAN's *American Presidents: Life Portraits* profile of Harry Truman

INDEX

INDEX

PICTURE CREDITS

Contributors

ARTHUR M. SCHLESINGER JR. holds the Albert Schweitzer Chair in the Humanities at the Graduate Center of the City University of New York. He is the author of more than a dozen books, including *The Age of Jackson*; *The Vital Center*; *The Age of Roosevelt* (3 vols.); *A Thousand Days: John F. Kennedy in the White House*; *Robert Kennedy and His Times*; *The Cycles of American History*; and *The Imperial Presidency*. Professor Schlesinger served as Special Assistant to President Kennedy (1961–63). His numerous awards include the Pulitzer Prize for History; the Pulitzer Prize for Biography; two National Book Awards; the Bancroft Prize; and the American Academy of Arts and Letters Gold Medal for History.

BARBARA SAFFER, a former college instructor, has Ph.D. degrees in biology and geology. She writes fiction and nonfiction for children, and has published books about geography, exploration, famous people, and historical events. Her Gifted and Talented Science Books are used in many schools, and her stories and articles have appeared in numerous children's magazines. Barbara lives in Birmingham, Alabama, with her family. For more information, visit her website at www.BarbaraSaffer.com.

.